CONTENTS

A C

Emily Sohn

illustrated by Steve Erwin

and Charles Barnett

www.raintreepublishers.co.uk
Visit our website to find out
more information about
Raintree books.

To order:
☎ Phone +44 (0) 1865 888066
🖷 Fax +44 (0) 1865 314091
🖳 Visit www.raintreepublishers.co.uk

Raintree is an imprint of Capstone Global Library Limited, a company incorporated in England and
Wales having its registered office at 7 Pilgrim Street, London EC4V 6LB
Registered company number: 6695882

Text © Capstone Press 2008
First published by Capstone Press in 2008
First published in hardback in the United Kingdom by Capstone Global Library in 2010
First published in paperback in the United Kingdom by Capstone Global Library in 2011
The moral rights of the proprietor have been asserted.

ISBN 978 1 4062 1457 4 (hardback)   ISBN 978 1 4062 1473 4 (paperback)
14 13 12 11 10   15 14 13 12 11

British Library Cataloguing in Publication Data
Sohn, Emily.
Forces and motion. -- (Graphic science)
531.1'1-dc22
A full catalogue record for this book is available from the British Library.

Art Director and Designer: Bob Lentz
Cover Artist: Tod Smith
Colourist: Krista Ward
UK Editor: Diyan Leake
UK Production: Alison Parsons
Originated by Capstone Global Library
Printed and bound in China by South China Printing Company Limited

Acknowledgements
The publisher would like to thank the following for permission to reproduce copyright material:
Corbis p. 19 (Jeffrey L. Rotman); Library of Congress p. 7; NASA p. 13 (JPL)

Disclaimer
All the Internet addresses (URLs) given in this book were valid at the time of going to press.
However, due to the dynamic nature of the Internet, some addresses may have changed, or sites may
have changed or ceased to exist since publication. While the publisher regrets any inconvenience this
may cause readers, no responsibility for any such changes can be accepted by the publisher.

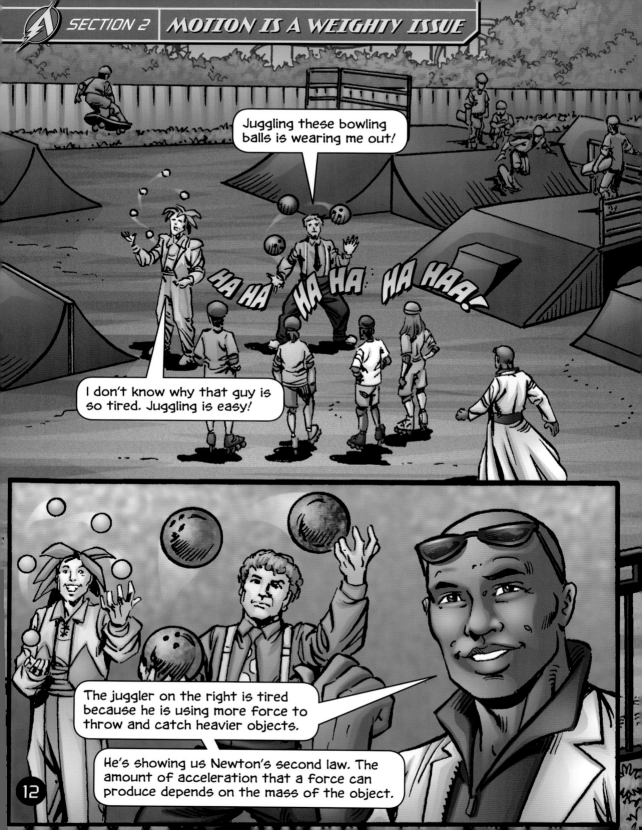

Whew!
Moving can be thrilling, but I need a break.
SNAP
SNAP
Hi, Alesha! What are you doing here?
Hello, Max! I'm taking notes for the science lesson I'm teaching later. Why are you just sitting there? Is something wrong?
Once I sit, sometimes it's hard to get moving again. But once I get going, I often can't stop.

What's mass, Uncle Max?

Mass is the amount of matter in an object. The bowling ball has more matter in it than the tennis ball, so it feels heavier.

Think about it. Which ball would be easier to juggle, Nick?

GRAVITATIONAL PULL

ACCESS GRANTED: MAX AXIOM

Weight is different from mass. Weight is determined by gravity's pull on an object. Each planet in our solar system has a different gravitational pull. If you travelled to each of the places below, your mass would always be the same, but your weight would be different. Multiply your weight by the number shown below each planet to find out how much you would weigh there. If you weigh 45 kg (100 lb.) on earth, you would weigh 17 kg (38 lb.) on Mars and 106 kg (236 lb.) on Jupiter.

VENUS
.88

MARS
.38

JUPITER
2.36

NEPTUNE
1.13

SATURN
.92

13

14

15

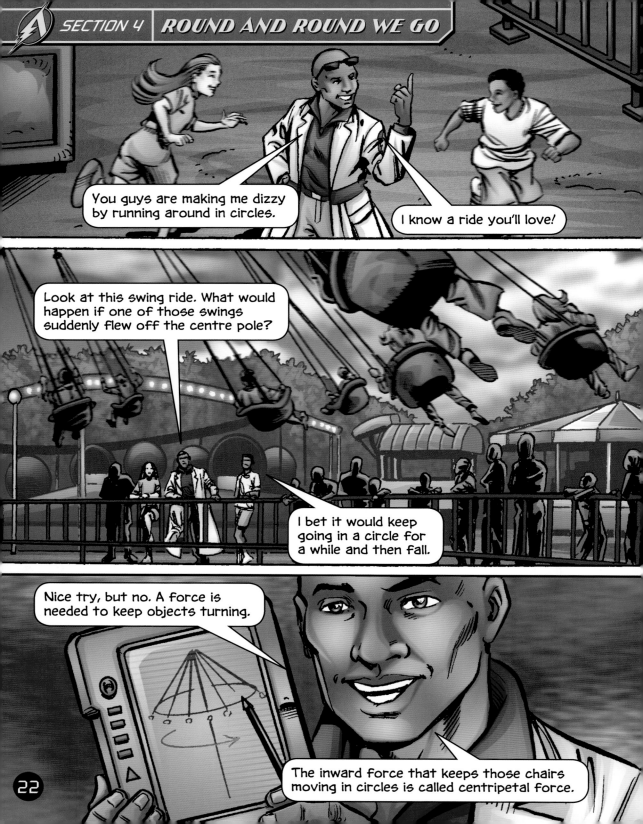

You guys are making me dizzy by running around in circles.

I know a ride you'll love!

Look at this swing ride. What would happen if one of those swings suddenly flew off the centre pole?

I bet it would keep going in a circle for a while and then fall.

Nice try, but no. A force is needed to keep objects turning.

The inward force that keeps those chairs moving in circles is called centripetal force.

22

But if the chain on a chair breaks, centripetal force no longer acts on the chair. The chair would fly off in a straight line.

Whoa!

Looks like it's our turn to ride.

Are you sure this ride is safe?

Whee!

Perfectly!

This ride is crazy, Uncle Max!

When we drop, watch the 2p coin I'm holding.

Whoa! The coin looks like it's just floating there.

It's magic!

Actually, it's science! We're in free fall, and so is the coin. We're all falling at the same speed, so the coin looks as weightless as we feel.

Do astronauts feel weightless in space because they are falling?

Yes. Orbit is a free fall in a circle.

EXIT

FORCES AND MOTION

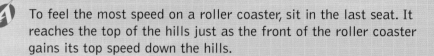

To feel the most speed on a roller coaster, sit in the last seat. It reaches the top of the hills just as the front of the roller coaster gains its top speed down the hills.

The motion of amusement park rides sometimes makes you feel sick. Swinging, spinning, or going around in loops causes your eyes and the fluid in your ears to send confusing signals to your brain. Your brain can't decide which way is up or down.

Forces that don't cause objects to move are balanced forces. A great example of balanced forces is the chair you're sitting on. As you sit on a chair, the force of gravity pulls your body downward. At the same time, the chair pushes upward on your body with an equal force. Without these forces in balance, the chair would break and you would find yourself sitting on the ground.

Friction actually slows down skydivers as they fall from an aeroplane. Air resistance is a form of friction that happens between air and an object moving through it. Even with air resistance, skydivers reach speeds of about 195 kilometres (120 miles) per hour during free falls.

The peregrine falcon is the fastest animal on earth. In a steep hunting dive, it can reach 320 kilometres (200 miles) per hour.

Inertia causes objects to stay at rest or keep moving until a force acts upon them. In a moving car, inertia can be dangerous. Your body moves at the same speed as the car. If the driver suddenly slams on the brakes, the car stops, but your body keeps moving forward. Your seat belt applies a force to stop your body's forward motion. It's the only thing that keeps you from flying through the windscreen.

 If you're looking for the fastest horse on the carousel, pick an outside horse. To complete the circle, it must cover more distance in the same amount of time as an inside horse.

MORE ABOUT

SUPER SCIENTIST

Real name: Maxwell Axiom
Height: 1.86 m (6 ft 1 in.)
Weight: 87 kg (13 st. 10 lb.)
Eyes: Brown   **Hair:** None

Super capabilities: Super intelligence; able to shrink to the size of an atom; sunglasses give X-ray vision; lab coat allows for travel through time and space.

Origin: Since birth, Max Axiom seemed destined for greatness. His mother, a marine biologist, taught her son about the mysteries of the sea. His father, a nuclear physicist and volunteer park warden, showed Max the wonders of the earth and sky.

One day, while Max was hiking in the hills, a megacharged lightning bolt struck him with blinding fury. When he awoke, he discovered a new-found energy and set out to learn as much about science as possible. He travelled the globe studying every aspect of the subject. Then he was ready to share his knowledge and new identity with the world. He had become Max Axiom, Super Scientist.

Glossary

acceleration change in speed of a moving body

balance state when forces are equal

centripetal force force that pulls an object turning in a circle inward toward the centre

friction force created when two objects rub together; friction slows down objects

gravity force that pulls objects with mass together. Gravity increases as the mass of objects increases or objects get closer. It pulls objects down toward the centre of the earth.

inertia an object's state in which the object stays at rest or keeps moving in the same direction until a greater force acts on the object

mass amount of material in an object

orbit path an object follows while circling another object in space

resistance force that opposes or slows the motion of an object. Friction is a form of resistance.

speed how fast something moves; the measure of the time it takes something to cover a certain distance

weight measurement of how heavy something is

Find Out More

Books

10 Experiments Your Teacher Never Told You About, Andrew Solway (Raintree, 2006)

The Extreme Zone, Paul Mason (Raintree, 2006)

Fantastic Forces series, Chris Oxlade (Heinemann Library, 2006)

Forces: The Ups and Downs, Wendy Sadler (Raintree, 2006)

Roller Coaster!, Paul Mason (Raintree, 2007)

The Science of Forces (Tabletop Scientist series), Steve Parker (Heinemann Library, 2005)

The Story Behind Gravity, Sean Price (Heinemann Library, 2009)

Websites

http://www.bbc.co.uk/schools /ks2bitesize/science/physical_processes.shtml
Log on to this website for activities and quizzes ("Forces I Action" and "Friction").

http://newsbbc.co.uk/cbbcnews
Enter "gravity" in the Search field to find out more about the effects of forces and motion on playground equipment, roller coasters, and space travel.

INDEX